The Constitution and the Declaration of Independence of the United States of America

Delegates of the Constitutional Convention
and
Thomas Jefferson

Edited by
Edna Faust

Delegates of the Constitutional Convention
and
Thomas Jefferson

Edna Faust
Historical Contexts

ISBN 10: 0692653902
ISBN-13: 978-0692653906

Non-Fiction—Constitution of the United States of America—
Declaration of Independence—Bill of Rights—Amendments of
Constitution

Originalist Edition

To everyone who supports the freedom and liberty of the United States of America—the constitution has been under attack by the radical left wing—and they claim it is a living document. The constitution is not alive, nor is it dead, but is a document meant to define the constitutional role of government. The left wing are trying to redefine the constitution so that it will fit their values— the values that represent tyranny and totalitarianism.

Contents

Foreward

From the time that the constitution was written, the framers envisioned a society of justice and society—to the extent of freedom and liberty, with a prosperous society. They knew when they agreed to the declaration of independence, that they were facing an uphill battle with the most powerful government that existed—the country of England and King George. The declaration of indepednece was primarily writtent to declare their grievances against the British government, in order to establish a society of freedom, liberty, and prosperity. The constitution was written in order to define that type of society, in order to help the people to understand what the government can and cannot do. It is an undersanding that these two documents define the role of government and what can be accomplished by the people. The role of government must be limited, but currently, it is the largest entity in the world, contributing to unlawful and unconstitutional acts across the oceans and domestically every single day of the year.

From time to time, a president who supports the constitution is elected to office, however, recent trends indicate that people elected into office do not uphold the constitution, both from the Republicans and the Democrats. It is true that Republicans support and uphold the constitution more than the Democrats, since the latter wants to change the constituion to a progressive living document. The constitution does not live and it is not dead. The constitution is amended when states feel something needs to be accomplished, such as term limits and the question of freedom. The constitution is not constantly changing like politicians and people want you to believe, but is meant to be intrepreted as it was written back in the eighteenth century.

Throughout the life of this country, the framers would be rolling in their graves, since the country and its leaders fail to follow the constitution itself. The government must follow the original intent of the constitution in order to live, prosper, and celebrate freedom and liberty, to the intent of its original meaning.

In this first edition of the constitution and the declaration of independence, you will see what the framers and founders meant and what they wanted to have a free and prosperous society. You will find the original constitution transcribed, the last ten articles of the joint resolution of 1789 to adopt the intial freedoms certain factions wanted (also known as the Bill of Rights), the regular amendments, and the declaration of independence.

This copy of the constitution includes commentary that describes what the original interpretation should follow. This copy will describe to you in detail what the words of the constituion meant when it was signed into law, as well as the bill of rights, and the rest of the amendments. You will find this copy of the constitution and the declaration of independence to have meaning of the original intention. This edition includes the full, amended copy of the constitution with notations and the declaration of independence. The interpretations of the original constitution and the bill of rights are described in originalist terminology, by textuality and intentionality, meaning that it is described as what the framers and the founders envisioned as a country of freedom, liberty, hopes, new dreams, and a prosperous society.

It is the interest of liberty and society to promote the original interpretation of the constitution, but that is often dismissed as dangerous, because certain politicians, as well as the government, fear liberty, freedom, and propserity. They rather have a communist state where everybody is controlled by a central government. Freedom and liberty is not a utopian society, nor is is some dystopian society, or even a communist state where everyone is equal. Freedom and liberty must thrive to promote the original intention of the constituion, as well as the original intention of the bill of rights. People must end this nonsense about supporting the establishing of a surveillance and police state, since the framers feared this, and the people who want to establish a surveillance and police state are the ones promoting the nonsense. Tyranny is bad and it must be stopped and prevented.

The Constitution

Editor
Edna Faust

Written by
The Delegates of the Constitutional Convention

Preamble

We the People of the United States, in Order to form a more perfect Union, establish Justice, insure domestic Tranquility, provide for the common defence, promote the general Welfare, and secure the Blessings of Liberty to ourselves and our Posterity, do ordain and establish this Constitution for the United States of America.

Article I

Section. 1.

All legislative Powers herein granted shall be vested in a Congress of the United States, which shall consist of a Senate and House of Representatives.

Section. 2.

The House of Representatives shall be composed of Members chosen every second Year by the People of the several States, and the Electors in each State shall have the Qualifications requisite for Electors of the most numerous Branch of the State Legislature.

No Person shall be a Representative who shall not have attained to the Age of twenty five Years, and been seven Years a Citizen of the United States, and who shall not, when elected, be an Inhabitant of that State in which he shall be chosen.

Representatives and direct Taxes shall be apportioned among the several States which may be included within this Union, according to their respective Numbers, which shall be determined by adding to the whole Number of free Persons, including those bound to Service for a Term of Years, and excluding Indians not taxed, three fifths of all other Persons. The actual Enumeration shall be made within three Years after the first Meeting of the Congress of the United States, and within every subsequent Term of ten Years, in such Manner as they shall by Law direct. The Number of Representatives shall not exceed one for every thirty Thousand, but each State shall have at Least one Representative; and until such enumeration shall be made, the State of New Hampshire shall be entitled to chuse three, Massachusetts eight, Rhode-Island and Providence Plantations one, Connecticut five, New-York six, New Jersey four, Pennsylvania eight, Delaware one, Maryland six, Virginia ten, North Carolina five, South Carolina five, and Georgia three.

When vacancies happen in the Representation from any State, the Executive Authority thereof shall issue Writs of Election to fill such Vacancies.

The House of Representatives shall chuse their Speaker and other Officers; and shall have the sole Power of Impeachment.

Section. 3.

The Senate of the United States shall be composed of two Senators from each State, chosen by the Legislature thereof, for six Years; and each Senator shall have one Vote.

Immediately after they shall be assembled in Consequence of the first Election, they shall be divided as equally as may be into three Classes. The Seats of the Senators of the first Class shall be vacated at the Expiration of the second Year, of the second Class at the Expiration of the fourth Year, and of the third Class at the Expiration of the sixth Year, so that one third may be chosen every second Year; and if Vacancies happen by Resignation, or otherwise, during the Recess of the Legislature of any State, the Executive thereof may make temporary Appointments until the next Meeting of the Legislature, which shall then fill such Vacancies.

No Person shall be a Senator who shall not have attained to the Age of thirty Years, and been nine Years a Citizen of the United States, and who shall not, when elected, be an Inhabitant of that State for which he shall be chosen.

The Vice President of the United States shall be President of the Senate, but shall have no Vote, unless they be equally divided.

The Senate shall chuse their other Officers, and also a President pro tempore, in the Absence of the Vice President, or when he shall exercise the Office of President of the United States.

The Senate shall have the sole Power to try all Impeachments. When sitting for that Purpose, they shall be on Oath or Affirmation. When the President of the United States is tried, the Chief Justice shall preside: And no Person shall be convicted without the Concurrence of two thirds of the Members present.

Judgment in Cases of Impeachment shall not extend further than to removal from Office, and disqualification to hold and enjoy any Office of honor, Trust or Profit under the United States: but the Party convicted shall nevertheless be liable and subject to Indictment, Trial, Judgment and Punishment, according to Law.

Section. 4.

The Times, Places and Manner of holding Elections for Senators and Representatives, shall be prescribed in each State by the Legislature thereof; but the Congress may at any time by Law make or alter such Regulations, except as to the Places of chusing Senators.

The Congress shall assemble at least once in every Year, and such Meeting shall be on the first Monday in December, unless they shall by Law appoint a different Day.

Section. 5.

Each House shall be the Judge of the Elections, Returns and Qualifications of its own Members, and a Majority of each shall constitute a Quorum to do Business; but a smaller Number may adjourn from day to day, and may be authorized to compel the Attendance of absent Members, in such Manner, and under such Penalties as each House may provide.

Each House may determine the Rules of its Proceedings, punish its Members for disorderly Behaviour, and, with the Concurrence of two thirds, expel a Member.

Each House shall keep a Journal of its Proceedings, and from time to time publish the same, excepting such Parts as may in their Judgment require Secrecy; and the Yeas and Nays of the Members of either House on any question shall, at the Desire of one fifth of those Present, be entered on the Journal.

Neither House, during the Session of Congress, shall, without the Consent of the other, adjourn for more than three days, nor to any other Place than that in which the two Houses shall be sitting.

Section. 6.

The Senators and Representatives shall receive a Compensation for their Services, to be ascertained by Law, and paid out of the Treasury of the United States. They shall in all Cases, except Treason, Felony and Breach of the Peace, be privileged from Arrest during their Attendance at the Session of their respective Houses, and in going to and returning from the same; and for any Speech or Debate in either House, they shall not be questioned in any other Place.

No Senator or Representative shall, during the Time for which he was elected, be appointed to any civil Office under the Authority of the United States, which shall have been created, or the Emoluments whereof shall have been encreased during such time; and no Person holding any Office under the United States, shall be a Member of either House during his Continuance in Office.

Section. 7.

All Bills for raising Revenue shall originate in the House of Representatives; but the Senate may propose or concur with Amendments as on other Bills.

Every Bill which shall have passed the House of Representatives and the Senate, shall, before it become a Law, be presented to the President of the United States; If he approve he shall sign it, but if not he shall return it, with his Objections to that House in which it shall have originated, who shall enter the Objections at large on their Journal, and proceed to reconsider it. If after such Reconsideration two thirds of that House shall agree to pass the Bill, it shall be sent, together with the Objections, to the other House, by which it shall likewise be reconsidered, and if approved by two thirds of that House, it shall become a Law. But in all such Cases the Votes of both Houses shall be determined by yeas and Nays, and the Names of the Persons voting for and against the Bill shall be entered on the Journal of each House respectively. If any Bill shall not be returned by the President within ten Days (Sundays excepted) after it shall have been presented to him, the Same shall be a Law, in like Manner as if he had signed it, unless the Congress by their Adjournment prevent its Return, in which Case it shall not be a Law.

Every Order, Resolution, or Vote to which the Concurrence of the Senate and House of Representatives may be necessary (except on a question of Adjournment) shall be presented to the President of the United States; and before the Same shall take Effect, shall be approved by him, or being disapproved by him, shall be repassed by two thirds of the Senate and House of Representatives, according to the Rules and Limitations prescribed in the Case of a Bill.

Section. 8.

The Congress shall have Power To lay and collect Taxes, Duties, Imposts and Excises, to pay the Debts and provide for the common Defence and general Welfare of the United States; but all Duties, Imposts and Excises shall be uniform throughout the United States;

To borrow Money on the credit of the United States;

To regulate Commerce with foreign Nations, and among the several States, and with the Indian Tribes;

To establish an uniform Rule of Naturalization, and uniform Laws on the subject of Bankruptcies throughout the United States;

To coin Money, regulate the Value thereof, and of foreign Coin, and fix the Standard of Weights and Measures;

To provide for the Punishment of counterfeiting the Securities and current Coin of the United States;

To establish Post Offices and post Roads;

To promote the Progress of Science and useful Arts, by securing for limited Times to Authors and Inventors the exclusive Right to their respective Writings and Discoveries;

To constitute Tribunals inferior to the supreme Court;

To define and punish Piracies and Felonies committed on the high Seas, and Offences against the Law of Nations;

To declare War, grant Letters of Marque and Reprisal, and make Rules concerning Captures on Land and Water;

To raise and support Armies, but no Appropriation of Money to that Use shall be for a longer Term than two Years;

To provide and maintain a Navy;

To make Rules for the Government and Regulation of the land and naval Forces;
To provide for calling forth the Militia to execute the Laws of the Union, suppress Insurrections and repel Invasions;

To provide for organizing, arming, and disciplining, the Militia, and for governing such Part of them as may be employed in the Service of the United States, reserving to the States respectively, the Appointment of the Officers, and the Authority of training the Militia according to the discipline prescribed by Congress;

To exercise exclusive Legislation in all Cases whatsoever, over such District (not exceeding ten Miles square) as may, by Cession of particular States, and the Acceptance of Congress, become the Seat of the Government of the United States, and to exercise like Authority over all Places purchased by the Consent of the Legislature of the State in which the Same shall be, for the Erection of Forts, Magazines, Arsenals, dock-Yards, and other needful Buildings;—And

To make all Laws which shall be necessary and proper for carrying into Execution the foregoing Powers, and all other Powers vested by this Constitution in the Government of the United States, or in any Department or Officer thereof.

Section. 9.

The Migration or Importation of such Persons as any of the States now existing shall think proper to admit, shall not be prohibited by the Congress prior to the Year one thousand eight hundred and eight, but a Tax or duty may be imposed on such Importation, not exceeding ten dollars for each Person.

The Privilege of the Writ of Habeas Corpus shall not be suspended, unless when in Cases of Rebellion or Invasion the public Safety may require it.

No Bill of Attainder or ex post facto Law shall be passed.

No Capitation, or other direct, Tax shall be laid, unless in Proportion to the Census or enumeration herein before directed to be taken.
No Tax or Duty shall be laid on Articles exported from any State.

No Preference shall be given by any Regulation of Commerce or Revenue to the Ports of one State over those of another: nor shall Vessels bound to, or from, one State, be obliged to enter, clear, or pay Duties in another.

No Money shall be drawn from the Treasury, but in Consequence of Appropriations made by Law; and a regular Statement and Account of the Receipts and Expenditures of all public Money shall be published from time to time.

No Title of Nobility shall be granted by the United States: And no Person holding any Office of Profit or Trust under them, shall, without the Consent of the Congress, accept of any present, Emolument, Office, or Title, of any kind whatever, from any King, Prince, or foreign State.

Section. 10.

No State shall enter into any Treaty, Alliance, or Confederation; grant Letters of Marque and Reprisal; coin Money; emit Bills of Credit; make any Thing but gold and silver Coin a Tender in Payment of Debts; pass any Bill of Attainder, ex post facto Law, or Law impairing the Obligation of Contracts, or grant any Title of Nobility.

No State shall, without the Consent of the Congress, lay any Imposts or Duties on Imports or Exports, except what may be absolutely necessary for executing it's inspection Laws: and the net Produce of all Duties and Imposts, laid by any State on Imports or Exports, shall be for the Use of the Treasury of the United States; and all such Laws shall be subject to the Revision and Controul of the Congress.

No State shall, without the Consent of Congress, lay any Duty of Tonnage, keep Troops, or Ships of War in time of Peace, enter into any Agreement or Compact with another State, or with a foreign Power, or engage in War, unless actually invaded, or in such imminent Danger as will not admit of delay.

Article II

Section. 1.

The executive Power shall be vested in a President of the United States of America. He shall hold his Office during the Term of four Years, and, together with the Vice President, chosen for the same Term, be elected, as follows

Each State shall appoint, in such Manner as the Legislature thereof may direct, a Number of Electors, equal to the whole Number of Senators and Representatives to which the State may be entitled in the Congress: but no Senator or Representative, or Person holding an Office of Trust or Profit under the United States, shall be appointed an Elector.

The Electors shall meet in their respective States, and vote by Ballot for two Persons, of whom one at least shall not be an Inhabitant of the same State with themselves. And they shall make a List of all the Persons voted for, and of the Number of Votes for each; which List they shall sign and certify, and transmit sealed to the Seat of the Government of the United States, directed to the President of the Senate. The President of the Senate shall, in the Presence of the Senate and House of Representatives, open all the Certificates, and the Votes shall then be counted. The Person having the greatest Number of Votes shall be the President, if such Number be a Majority of the whole Number of Electors appointed; and if there be more than one who have such Majority, and have an equal Number of Votes, then the House of Representatives shall immediately chuse by Ballot one of them for President; and if no Person have a Majority, then from the five highest on the List the said House shall in like Manner chuse the President. But in chusing the President, the Votes shall be taken by States, the Representation from each State having one Vote; A quorum for this Purpose shall consist of a Member or Members from two thirds of the States, and a Majority of all the States shall be necessary to a Choice. In every Case, after the Choice of the President, the Person having the greatest Number of Votes of the

Electors shall be the Vice President. But if there should remain two or more who have equal Votes, the Senate shall chuse from them by Ballot the Vice President.

The Congress may determine the Time of chusing the Electors, and the Day on which they shall give their Votes; which Day shall be the same throughout the United States.

No Person except a natural born Citizen, or a Citizen of the United States, at the time of the Adoption of this Constitution, shall be eligible to the Office of President; neither shall any Person be eligible to that Office who shall not have attained to the Age of thirty five Years, and been fourteen Years a Resident within the United States.

In Case of the Removal of the President from Office, or of his Death, Resignation, or Inability to discharge the Powers and Duties of the said Office, the Same shall devolve on the Vice President, and the Congress may by Law provide for the Case of Removal, Death, Resignation or Inability, both of the President and Vice President, declaring what Officer shall then act as President, and such Officer shall act accordingly, until the Disability be removed, or a President shall be elected.

The President shall, at stated Times, receive for his Services, a Compensation, which shall neither be encreased nor diminished during the Period for which he shall have been elected, and he shall not receive within that Period any other Emolument from the United States, or any of them.

Before he enter on the Execution of his Office, he shall take the following Oath or Affirmation:—"I do solemnly swear (or affirm) that I will faithfully execute the Office of President of the United States, and will to the best of my Ability, preserve, protect and defend the Constitution of the United States."

Section. 2.

The President shall be Commander in Chief of the Army and Navy of the United States, and of the Militia of the several States, when called into the actual Service of the United States; he may require the Opinion, in writing, of the principal Officer in each of the executive Departments, upon any Subject relating to the Duties of their respective Offices, and he shall have Power to grant Reprieves and Pardons for Offences against the United States, except in Cases of Impeachment.

He shall have Power, by and with the Advice and Consent of the Senate, to make Treaties, provided two thirds of the Senators present concur; and he shall nominate, and by and with the Advice and Consent of the Senate, shall appoint Ambassadors, other public Ministers and Consuls, Judges of the supreme Court, and all other Officers of the United States, whose Appointments are not herein otherwise provided for, and which shall be established by Law: but the Congress may by Law vest the Appointment of such inferior Officers, as they think proper, in the President alone, in the Courts of Law, or in the Heads of Departments.

The President shall have Power to fill up all Vacancies that may happen during the Recess of the Senate, by granting Commissions which shall expire at the End of their next Session.

Section. 3.

He shall from time to time give to the Congress Information of the State of the Union, and recommend to their Consideration such Measures as he shall judge necessary and expedient; he may, on extraordinary Occasions, convene both Houses, or either of them, and in Case of Disagreement between them, with Respect to the Time of Adjournment, he may adjourn them to such Time as he shall think proper; he shall receive Ambassadors and other public Ministers; he shall take Care that the Laws be faithfully executed, and shall Commission all the Officers of the United States.

Section. 4.

The President, Vice President and all civil Officers of the United States, shall be removed from Office on Impeachment for, and Conviction of, Treason, Bribery, or other high Crimes and Misdemeanors.

Article III

Section. 1.

The judicial Power of the United States, shall be vested in one supreme Court, and in such inferior Courts as the Congress may from time to time ordain and establish. The Judges, both of the supreme and inferior Courts, shall hold their Offices during good Behaviour, and shall, at stated Times, receive for their Services, a Compensation, which shall not be diminished during their Continuance in Office.

Section. 2.

The judicial Power shall extend to all Cases, in Law and Equity, arising under this Constitution, the Laws of the United States, and Treaties made, or which shall be made, under their Authority;—to all Cases affecting Ambassadors, other public Ministers and Consuls;—to all Cases of admiralty and maritime Jurisdiction;—to Controversies to which the United States shall be a Party;—to Controversies between two or more States;— between a State and Citizens of another State,—between Citizens of different States,— between Citizens of the same State claiming Lands under Grants of different States, and between a State, or the Citizens thereof, and foreign States, Citizens or Subjects.

In all Cases affecting Ambassadors, other public Ministers and Consuls, and those in which a State shall be Party, the supreme Court shall have original Jurisdiction. In all the other Cases before mentioned, the supreme Court shall have appellate Jurisdiction, both as to Law and Fact, with such Exceptions, and under such Regulations as the Congress shall make.

The Trial of all Crimes, except in Cases of Impeachment, shall be by Jury; and such Trial shall be held in the State where the said Crimes shall have been committed; but when not committed within any State, the Trial shall be at such Place or Places as the Congress may by Law have directed.

Section. 3.

Treason against the United States, shall consist only in levying War against them, or in adhering to their Enemies, giving them Aid and Comfort. No Person shall be convicted of Treason unless on the Testimony of two Witnesses to the same overt Act, or on Confession in open Court.

The Congress shall have Power to declare the Punishment of Treason, but no Attainder of Treason shall work Corruption of Blood, or Forfeiture except during the Life of the Person attainted.

Article. IV

Section. 1.

Full Faith and Credit shall be given in each State to the public Acts, Records, and judicial Proceedings of every other State. And the Congress may by general Laws prescribe the Manner in which such Acts, Records and Proceedings shall be proved, and the Effect thereof.

Section. 2.

The Citizens of each State shall be entitled to all Privileges and Immunities of Citizens in the several States.

A Person charged in any State with Treason, Felony, or other Crime, who shall flee from Justice, and be found in another State, shall on Demand of the executive Authority of the State from which he fled, be delivered up, to be removed to the State having Jurisdiction of the Crime.

No Person held to Service or Labour in one State, under the Laws thereof, escaping into another, shall, in Consequence of any Law or Regulation therein, be discharged from such Service or Labour, but shall be delivered up on Claim of the Party to whom such Service or Labour may be due.

Section. 3.

New States may be admitted by the Congress into this Union; but no new State shall be formed or erected within the Jurisdiction of any other State; nor any State be formed by the Junction of two or more States, or Parts of States, without the Consent of the Legislatures of the States concerned as well as of the Congress.

The Congress shall have Power to dispose of and make all needful Rules and Regulations respecting the Territory or other Property belonging to the United States; and nothing in this Constitution shall be so construed as to Prejudice any Claims of the United States, or of any particular State.

Section. 4.

The United States shall guarantee to every State in this Union a Republican Form of Government, and shall protect each of them against Invasion; and on Application of the Legislature, or of the Executive (when the Legislature cannot be convened), against domestic Violence.

Article. V

The Congress, whenever two thirds of both Houses shall deem it necessary, shall propose Amendments to this Constitution, or, on the Application of the Legislatures of two thirds of the several States, shall call a Convention for proposing Amendments, which, in either Case, shall be valid to all Intents and Purposes, as Part of this Constitution, when ratified by the Legislatures of three fourths of the several States, or by Conventions in three fourths thereof, as the one or the other Mode of Ratification may be proposed by the Congress; Provided that no Amendment which may be made prior to the Year One thousand eight hundred and eight shall in any Manner affect the first and fourth Clauses in the Ninth Section of the first Article; and that no State, without its Consent, shall be deprived of its equal Suffrage in the Senate.

Article. VI

All Debts contracted and Engagements entered into, before the Adoption of this Constitution, shall be as valid against the United States under this Constitution, as under the Confederation.

This Constitution, and the Laws of the United States which shall be made in Pursuance thereof; and all Treaties made, or which shall be made, under the Authority of the United States, shall be the supreme Law of the Land; and the Judges in every State shall be bound thereby, any Thing in the Constitution or Laws of any State to the Contrary notwithstanding.

The Senators and Representatives before mentioned, and the Members of the several State Legislatures, and all executive and judicial Officers, both of the United States and of the several States, shall be bound by Oath or Affirmation, to support this Constitution; but no religious Test shall ever be required as a Qualification to any Office or public Trust under the United States.

Article VII

The Ratification of the Conventions of nine States, shall be sufficient for the Establishment of this Constitution between the States so ratifying the Same.

DONE in Convention by the Unanimous Consent of the States present the Seventeenth Day of September in the Year of our Lord one thousand seven hundred and Eighty seven and of the Independence of the United States of America the Twelfth. In WITNESS whereof We have hereunto subscribed our Names,

George Washington
President and deputy from Virginia

Delaware
George Read
Gunning Bedford, Jr.
John Dickinson
Richard Bassett
Jacob Broom

Maryland
James McHenry
Daniel of St Thomas Jenifer
Daniel Carroll

Virginia
John Blair
James Madison, Jr.
North Carolina
William Blount
Richard Dobbs Spaight, Sr.
Hugh Williamson

South Carolina
John Rutledge
Charles Cotesworth Pinckney
Charles Pinckney
Pierce Butler

Georgia
William Few
Abraham Baldwin

New Hampshire
John Langdon
Nicholas Gilman

Massachusetts
Nathaniel Gorham
Rufus King
Connecticut
William. Samuel. Johnson
Roger Sherman

New York
Alexander Hamilton

New Jersey
William Livingston
David Brearley
William. Paterson
Jonathan Dayton

Pennsylvania
Benjamin Franklin
Thomas Mifflin
Robert Morris
George Clymer
Thomas Fitzsimons
Jared Ingersoll
James Wilson
Gouverneur Morris

Bill of Rights

Editor
Edna Faust

Written by
James Madison

First Amendment

Article the third

Congress shall make no law respecting an establishment of religion, or prohibiting the free exercise thereof; or abridging the freedom of speech, or of the press; or the right of the people peaceably to assemble, and to petition the Government for a redress of grievances.

Second Amendment

Article the fourth

A well-regulated Militia, being necessary to the security of a free State, the right of the people to keep and bear Arms, shall not be infringed.

Third Amendment

Article the fifth

No Soldier shall, in time of peace be quartered in any house, without the consent of the Owner, nor in time of war, but in a manner to be prescribed by law.

Fourth Amendment

Article the sixth

The right of the people to be secure in their persons, houses, papers, and effects, against unreasonable searches and seizures, shall not be violated, and no Warrants shall issue, but upon probable cause, supported by Oath or affirmation, and particularly describing the place to be searched, and the persons or things to be seized.

Fifth Amendment

Article the seventh

No person shall be held to answer for a capital, or otherwise infamous crime, unless on a presentment or indictment of a Grand Jury, except in cases arising in the land or naval forces, or in the Militia, when in actual service in time of War or public danger; nor shall any person be subject for the same offence to be twice put in jeopardy of life or limb; nor shall be compelled in any criminal case to be a witness against himself, nor be deprived of life, liberty, or property, without due process of law; nor shall private property be taken for public use, without just compensation.

Sixth Amendment

Article the eighth
In all criminal prosecutions, the accused shall enjoy the right to a speedy and public trial, by an impartial jury of the State and district wherein the crime shall have been committed, which district shall have been previously ascertained by law, and to be informed of the nature and cause of the accusation; to be confronted with the witnesses against him; to have compulsory process for obtaining witnesses in his favor, and to have the Assistance of Counsel for his defence.

Seventh Amendment

Article the ninth
In suits at common law, where the value in controversy shall exceed twenty dollars, the right of trial by jury shall be preserved, and no fact tried by a jury, shall be otherwise re-examined in any Court of the United States, than according to the rules of the common law.

Eight Amendment

Article the tenth
Excessive bail shall not be required, nor excessive fines imposed, nor cruel and unusual punishments inflicted.

Ninth Amendment

Article the eleventh
The enumeration in the Constitution, of certain rights, shall not be construed to deny or disparage others retained by the people.

Tenth Amendment

Article the twelfth
The powers not delegated to the United States by the Constitution, nor prohibited by it to the States, are reserved to the States respectively, or to the people.

ATTEST,

Frederick Augustus Muhlenberg,
Speaker of the House of Representatives

John Adams,
Vice-President of the United States and President of the Senate

John Beckley,
Clerk of the House of Representatives

Samuel Allyne Otis
Secretary of the Senate

Amendments to the Constitution

11-27

Editor
Edna Faust

The States of the Union

Eleventh Amendment

Note: Article III, section 2, of the Constitution was modified by amendment 11.

The Judicial power of the United States shall not be construed to extend to any suit in law or equity, commenced or prosecuted against one of the United States by Citizens of another State, or by Citizens or Subjects of any Foreign State.

Twelfth Amendment

Note: A portion of Article II, section 1 of the Constitution was superseded by the 12th amendment.

The Electors shall meet in their respective states and vote by ballot for President and Vice-President, one of whom, at least, shall not be an inhabitant of the same state with themselves; they shall name in their ballots the person voted for as President, and in distinct ballots the person voted for as Vice-President, and they shall make distinct lists of all persons voted for as President, and of all persons voted for as Vice-President, and of the number of votes for each, which lists they shall sign and certify, and transmit sealed to the seat of the government of the United States, directed to the President of the Senate; -- the President of the Senate shall, in the presence of the Senate and House of Representatives, open all the certificates and the votes shall then be counted; -- The person having the greatest number of votes for President, shall be the President, if such number be a majority of the whole number of Electors appointed; and if no person have such majority, then from the persons having the highest numbers not exceeding three on the list of those voted for as President, the House of Representatives shall choose immediately, by ballot, the President. But in choosing the President, the votes shall be taken by states, the representation from each state having one vote; a quorum for this purpose shall consist of a member or members from two-thirds of the states, and a majority of all the states shall be necessary to a choice. [And if the House of Representatives shall not choose a President whenever the right of choice shall devolve upon them, before the fourth day of March next following, then the Vice-President shall act as President, as in case of the death or other constitutional disability of the President. --]* The person having the greatest number of votes as Vice-President, shall be the Vice-President, if such number be a majority of the whole number of Electors appointed, and if no person have a majority, then from the two highest numbers on the list, the Senate shall choose the Vice-President; a quorum for the purpose shall consist of two-thirds of the whole number of Senators, and a majority of the whole number shall be necessary to a choice. But no person constitutionally ineligible to the office of President shall be eligible to that of Vice-President of the United States.

*Superseded by section 3 of the 20th amendment.

Thirteenth Amendment
Note: A portion of Article IV, section 2, of the Constitution was superseded by the 13th amendment.

Section 1.
Neither slavery nor involuntary servitude, except as a punishment for crime whereof the party shall have been duly convicted, shall exist within the United States, or any place subject to their jurisdiction.

Section 2.
Congress shall have power to enforce this article by appropriate legislation.

Fourteenth Amendment
Note: Article I, section 2, of the Constitution was modified by section 2 of the 14th amendment.

Section 1.
All persons born or naturalized in the United States, and subject to the jurisdiction thereof, are citizens of the United States and of the State wherein they reside. No State shall make or enforce any law which shall abridge the privileges or immunities of citizens of the United States; nor shall any State deprive any person of life, liberty, or property, without due process of law; nor deny to any person within its jurisdiction the equal protection of the laws.

Section 2.

Representatives shall be apportioned among the several States according to their respective numbers, counting the whole number of persons in each State, excluding Indians not taxed. But when the right to vote at any election for the choice of electors for President and Vice-President of the United States, Representatives in Congress, the Executive and Judicial officers of a State, or the members of the Legislature thereof, is denied to any of the male inhabitants of such State, being twenty-one years of age,* and citizens of the United States, or in any way abridged, except for participation in rebellion, or other crime, the basis of representation therein shall be reduced in the proportion which the number of such male citizens shall bear to the whole number of male citizens twenty-one years of age in such State.

Section 3.

No person shall be a Senator or Representative in Congress, or elector of President and Vice-President, or hold any office, civil or military, under the United States, or under any State, who, having previously taken an oath, as a member of Congress, or as an officer of the United States, or as a member of any State legislature, or as an executive or judicial officer of any State, to support the Constitution of the United States, shall have engaged in insurrection or rebellion against the same, or given aid or comfort to the enemies thereof. But Congress may by a vote of two-thirds of each House, remove such disability.

Section 4.

The validity of the public debt of the United States, authorized by law, including debts incurred for payment of pensions and bounties for services in suppressing insurrection or rebellion, shall not be questioned. But neither the United States nor any State shall assume or pay any debt or obligation incurred in aid of insurrection or rebellion against the United States, or any claim for the loss or emancipation of any slave; but all such debts, obligations and claims shall be held illegal and void.

Section 5.
The Congress shall have the power to enforce, by appropriate legislation, the provisions of this article.

*Changed by section 1 of the 26th amendment.

Fifteenth Amendment

Section 1.
The right of citizens of the United States to vote shall not be denied or abridged by the United States or by any State on account of race, color, or previous condition of servitude--

Section 2.
The Congress shall have the power to enforce this article by appropriate legislation.

Sixteenth Amendment
Note: Article I, section 9, of the Constitution was modified by amendment 16.

The Congress shall have power to lay and collect taxes on incomes, from whatever source derived, without apportionment among the several States, and without regard to any census or enumeration.

Seventeenth Amendment
Note: Article I, section 3, of the Constitution was modified by the 17th amendment.

The Senate of the United States shall be composed of two Senators from each State, elected by the people thereof, for six years; and each Senator shall have one vote. The electors in each State shall have the qualifications requisite for electors of the most numerous branch of the State legislatures.

When vacancies happen in the representation of any State in the Senate, the executive authority of such State shall issue writs of election to fill such vacancies: Provided, That the legislature of any State may empower the executive thereof to make temporary appointments until the people fill the vacancies by election as the legislature may direct.

This amendment shall not be so construed as to affect the election or term of any Senator chosen before it becomes valid as part of the Constitution.

Eighteenth Amendment

Section 1.
After one year from the ratification of this article the manufacture, sale, or transportation of intoxicating liquors within, the importation thereof into, or the exportation thereof from the United States and all territory subject to the jurisdiction thereof for beverage purposes is hereby prohibited.

Section 2.
The Congress and the several States shall have concurrent power to enforce this article by appropriate legislation.

Section 3.
This article shall be inoperative unless it shall have been ratified as an amendment to the Constitution by the legislatures of the several States, as provided in the Constitution, within seven years from the date of the submission hereof to the States by the Congress.

Nineteenth Amendment

The right of citizens of the United States to vote shall not be denied or abridged by the United States or by any State on account of sex.

Congress shall have power to enforce this article by appropriate legislation.

Twentieth Amendment

Note: Article I, section 4, of the Constitution was modified by section 2 of this amendment. In addition, a portion of the 12th amendment was superseded by section 3.

Section 1.

The terms of the President and the Vice President shall end at noon on the 20th day of January, and the terms of Senators and Representatives at noon on the 3d day of January, of the years in which such terms would have ended if this article had not been ratified; and the terms of their successors shall then begin.

Section 2.

The Congress shall assemble at least once in every year, and such meeting shall begin at noon on the 3d day of January, unless they shall by law appoint a different day.

Section 3.

If, at the time fixed for the beginning of the term of the President, the President elect shall have died, the Vice President elect shall become President. If a President shall not have been chosen before the time fixed for the beginning of his term, or if the President elect shall have failed to qualify, then the Vice President elect shall act as President until a President shall have qualified; and the Congress may by law provide for the case wherein neither a President elect nor a Vice President elect shall have qualified, declaring who shall then act as President, or the manner in which one who is to act shall be selected, and such person shall act accordingly until a President or Vice President shall have qualified.

Section 4.

The Congress may by law provide for the case of the death of any of the persons from whom the House of Representatives may choose a President whenever the right of choice shall have devolved upon them, and for the case of the death of any of the persons from whom the Senate may choose a Vice President whenever the right of choice shall have devolved upon them.

Section 5.
Sections 1 and 2 shall take effect on the 15th day of October following the ratification of this article.

Section 6.
This article shall be inoperative unless it shall have been ratified as an amendment to the Constitution by the legislatures of three-fourths of the several States within seven years from the date of its submission.

Twenty-First Amendment

Section 1.
The eighteenth article of amendment to the Constitution of the United States is hereby repealed.

Section 2.
The transportation or importation into any State, Territory, or possession of the United States for delivery or use therein of intoxicating liquors, in violation of the laws thereof, is hereby prohibited.

Section 3.
This article shall be inoperative unless it shall have been ratified as an amendment to the Constitution by conventions in the several States, as provided in the Constitution, within seven years from the date of the submission hereof to the States by the Congress.

Twenty-Second Amendment

Section 1.
No person shall be elected to the office of the President more than twice, and no person who has held the office of President, or acted as President, for more than two years of a term to which some other person was elected President shall be elected to the office of the President more than once. But this Article shall not apply to any person holding the office of President when this Article was

proposed by the Congress, and shall not prevent any person who may be holding the office of President, or acting as President, during the term within which this Article becomes operative from holding the office of President or acting as President during the remainder of such term.

Section 2.
This article shall be inoperative unless it shall have been ratified as an amendment to the Constitution by the legislatures of three-fourths of the several States within seven years from the date of its submission to the States by the Congress.

Twenty-Third Amendment

Section 1.
The District constituting the seat of Government of the United States shall appoint in such manner as the Congress may direct:

A number of electors of President and Vice President equal to the whole number of Senators and Representatives in Congress to which the District would be entitled if it were a State, but in no event more than the least populous State; they shall be in addition to those appointed by the States, but they shall be considered, for the purposes of the election of President and Vice President, to be electors appointed by a State; and they shall meet in the District and perform such duties as provided by the twelfth article of amendment.

Section 2.
The Congress shall have power to enforce this article by appropriate legislation.

Twenty-Fourth Amendment

Section 1.
The right of citizens of the United States to vote in any primary or other election for President or Vice President, for electors for President or Vice President, or for Senator or Representative in

Congress, shall not be denied or abridged by the United States or any State by reason of failure to pay any poll tax or other tax.

Section 2.
The Congress shall have power to enforce this article by appropriate legislation.

Twenty-Fifth Amendment
Note: Article II, section 1, of the Constitution was affected by the 25th amendment.

Section 1.
In case of the removal of the President from office or of his death or resignation, the Vice President shall become President.

Section 2.
Whenever there is a vacancy in the office of the Vice President, the President shall nominate a Vice President who shall take office upon confirmation by a majority vote of both Houses of Congress.

Section 3.
Whenever the President transmits to the President pro tempore of the Senate and the Speaker of the House of Representatives his written declaration that he is unable to discharge the powers and duties of his office, and until he transmits to them a written declaration to the contrary, such powers and duties shall be discharged by the Vice President as Acting President.

Section 4.
Whenever the Vice President and a majority of either the principal officers of the executive departments or of such other body as Congress may by law provide, transmit to the President pro tempore of the Senate and the Speaker of the House of Representatives their written declaration that the President is unable to discharge the powers and duties of his office, the Vice President shall immediately assume the powers and duties of the office as Acting President.

Thereafter, when the President transmits to the President pro tempore of the Senate and the Speaker of the House of Representatives his written declaration that no inability exists, he shall resume the powers and duties of his office unless the Vice President and a majority of either the principal officers of the executive department or of such other body as Congress may by law provide, transmit within four days to the President pro tempore of the Senate and the Speaker of the House of Representatives their written declaration that the President is unable to discharge the powers and duties of his office. Thereupon Congress shall decide the issue, assembling within forty-eight hours for that purpose if not in session. If the Congress, within twenty-one days after receipt of the latter written declaration, or, if Congress is not in session, within twenty-one days after Congress is required to assemble, determines by two-thirds vote of both Houses that the President is unable to discharge the powers and duties of his office, the Vice President shall continue to discharge the same as Acting President; otherwise, the President shall resume the powers and duties of his office.

Twenty-Sixth Amendment

Note: Amendment 14, section 2, of the Constitution was modified by section 1 of the 26th amendment.

Section 1.
The right of citizens of the United States, who are eighteen years of age or older, to vote shall not be denied or abridged by the United States or by any State on account of age.

Section 2.
The Congress shall have power to enforce this article by appropriate legislation.

Twenty-Seventh Amendment

No law, varying the compensation for the services of the Senators and Representatives, shall take effect, until an election of Representatives shall have intervened.

Declaration of Independence

Editor
Edna Faust

Written by
Thomas Jefferson

Declaration of Independence

IN CONGRESS, July 4, 1776.

The unanimous Declaration of the thirteen united States of America,

When in the Course of human events, it becomes necessary for one people to dissolve the political bands which have connected them with another, and to assume among the powers of the earth, the separate and equal station to which the Laws of Nature and of Nature's God entitle them, a decent respect to the opinions of mankind requires that they should declare the causes which impel them to the separation.

We hold these truths to be self-evident, that all men are created equal, that they are endowed by their Creator with certain unalienable Rights, that among these are Life, Liberty and the pursuit of Happiness.--That to secure these rights, Governments are instituted among Men, deriving their just powers from the consent of the governed, --That whenever any Form of Government becomes destructive of these ends, it is the Right of the People to alter or to abolish it, and to institute new Government, laying its foundation on such principles and organizing its powers in such form, as to them shall seem most likely to effect their Safety and Happiness. Prudence, indeed, will dictate that Governments long established should not be changed for light and transient causes; and accordingly all experience hath shewn, that mankind are more disposed to suffer, while evils are sufferable, than to right themselves by abolishing the forms to which they are accustomed. But when a long train of abuses and usurpations, pursuing invariably the same Object evinces a design to reduce them under absolute Despotism, it is their right, it is their duty, to throw off such Government, and to provide new Guards for their future security.--Such has been the patient sufferance of these Colonies; and such is now the necessity which constrains them to alter their former Systems of Government. The history of the present King of Great Britain is a history of repeated injuries and usurpations, all having in direct object the establishment of an absolute Tyranny over these States. To prove this, let Facts be submitted to a candid world.

He has refused his Assent to Laws, the most wholesome and necessary for the public good.
He has forbidden his Governors to pass Laws of immediate and pressing importance, unless suspended in their operation till his Assent should be obtained; and when so suspended, he has utterly neglected to attend to them.
He has refused to pass other Laws for the accommodation of large districts of people, unless those people would relinquish the right of Representation in the Legislature, a right inestimable to them and formidable to tyrants only.

He has called together legislative bodies at places unusual, uncomfortable, and distant from the depository of their public Records, for the sole purpose of fatiguing them into compliance with his measures.

He has dissolved Representative Houses repeatedly, for opposing with manly firmness his invasions on the rights of the people.
He has refused for a long time, after such dissolutions, to cause others to be elected; whereby the Legislative powers, incapable of Annihilation, have returned to the People at large for their exercise; the State remaining in the meantime exposed to all the dangers of invasion from without, and convulsions within.
He has endeavoured to prevent the population of these States; for that purpose obstructing the Laws for Naturalization of Foreigners; refusing to pass others to encourage their migrations hither, and raising the conditions of new Appropriations of Lands.

He has obstructed the Administration of Justice, by refusing his Assent to Laws for establishing Judiciary powers.
He has made Judges dependent on his Will alone, for the tenure of their offices, and the amount and payment of their salaries.

He has erected a multitude of New Offices, and sent hither swarms of Officers to harass our people, and eat out their substance.

He has kept among us, in times of peace, Standing Armies without the Consent of our legislatures.

He has affected to render the Military independent of and superior to the Civil power.
He has combined with others to subject us to a jurisdiction foreign to our constitution, and unacknowledged by our laws; giving his Assent to their Acts of pretended Legislation:

For Quartering large bodies of armed troops among us:

For protecting them, by a mock Trial, from punishment for any Murders which they should commit on the Inhabitants of these States:

For cutting off our Trade with all parts of the world:

For imposing Taxes on us without our Consent:
For depriving us in many cases, of the benefits of Trial by Jury:
For transporting us beyond Seas to be tried for pretended offences

For abolishing the free System of English Laws in a neighbouring Province, establishing therein an Arbitrary government, and enlarging its Boundaries so as to render it at once an example and fit instrument for introducing the same absolute rule into these Colonies:

For taking away our Charters, abolishing our most valuable Laws, and altering fundamentally the Forms of our Governments:

For suspending our own Legislatures, and declaring themselves invested with power to legislate for us in all cases whatsoever.

He has abdicated Government here, by declaring us out of his Protection and waging War against us.

He has plundered our seas, ravaged our Coasts, burnt our towns, and destroyed the lives of our people.

He is at this time transporting large Armies of foreign Mercenaries to complete the works of death, desolation and tyranny, already begun with circumstances of Cruelty & perfidy scarcely paralleled in the most barbarous ages, and totally unworthy the Head of a civilized nation.

He has constrained our fellow Citizens taken Captive on the high Seas to bear Arms against their Country, to become the executioners of their friends and Brethren, or to fall themselves by their Hands.

He has excited domestic insurrections amongst us, and has endeavoured to bring on the inhabitants of our frontiers, the merciless Indian Savages, whose known rule of warfare, is an undistinguished destruction of all ages, sexes and conditions.

In every stage of these Oppressions We have Petitioned for Redress in the most humble terms: Our repeated Petitions have been answered only by repeated injury. A Prince whose character is thus marked by every act which may define a Tyrant, is unfit to be the ruler of a free people.

Nor have We been wanting in attentions to our British brethren. We have warned them from time to time of attempts by their legislature to extend an unwarrantable jurisdiction over us. We have reminded them of the circumstances of our emigration and settlement here. We have appealed to their native justice and magnanimity, and we have conjured them by the ties of our common kindred to disavow these usurpations, which, would inevitably interrupt our connections and correspondence. They too have been deaf to the voice of justice and of consanguinity. We must, therefore, acquiesce in the necessity, which denounces our Separation, and hold them, as we hold the rest of mankind, Enemies in War, in Peace Friends.

We, therefore, the Representatives of the united States of America, in General Congress, Assembled, appealing to the Supreme Judge of the world for the rectitude of our intentions, do, in the Name, and by Authority of the good People of these Colonies, solemnly publish and declare, That these United Colonies are, and of Right ought to be Free and Independent States; that they are Absolved from all Allegiance to the British Crown, and that all political connection between them and the State of Great Britain, is and ought to be totally dissolved; and that as Free and Independent States, they have full Power to levy War, conclude Peace, contract Alliances, establish Commerce, and to do all other Acts and Things which Independent States may of right do. And for the support of this Declaration, with a firm reliance on the protection of divine Providence, we mutually pledge to each other our Lives, our Fortunes and our sacred Honor.

George Taylor
James Wilson
George Ross

Georgia
Button Gwinnett
Lyman Hall
George Walton

North Carolina
William Hooper
Joseph Hewes
John Penn

South Carolina
Edward Rutledge
Thomas Heyward, Jr.
Thomas Lynch, Jr.
Arthur Middleton

Massachusetts
John Hancock

Maryland
Samuel Chase
William Paca
Thomas Stone
Charles Carroll of Carrollton

Virginia
George Wythe
Richard Henry Lee
Thomas Jefferson
Benjamin Harrison
Thomas Nelson, Jr.
Francis Lightfoot Lee
Carter Braxton

Pennsylvania
Robert Morris
Benjamin Rush
Benjamin Franklin
John Morton
George Clymer
James Smith

Delaware
Caesar Rodney
George Read
Thomas McKean

New York
William Floyd
Philip Livingston
Francis Lewis
Lewis Morris

New Jersey
Richard Stockton
John Witherspoon
Francis Hopkinson
John Hart
Abraham Clark

New Hampshire
Josiah Bartlett
William Whipple

Massachusetts
Samuel Adams
John Adams
Robert Treat Paine
Elbridge Gerry

Rhode Island
Stephen Hopkins
William Ellery

Connecticut
Roger Sherman
Samuel Huntington
William Williams
Oliver Wolcott

New Hampshire
Matthew Thornton

Constitutional Interpretation

The Constitution as it was Originally meant to be Interpreted

Written by
Edna Faust

Preamble Originalist Interpretation

Originalist Interpretation

For the framers of the constitution, they envisioned the United States of America as a new hope for better society, with more freedom, liberty, dreams, and prosperity more than any other country existed. They believed the rights were ordained by God, not by government. In the preamble to the constitution, the framers wanted to create a perfect but not perfect society in which freedom, liberty, and justice flourished. They wanted to establish a society of peace, not war, to help the people in the time of need, in order to live in a free and better society that does not promote hatred, hostility, or bigotry towards the rest of society. General welfare did not mean mandatory, but a crucial step to help and take care of the people of the new country and society. Making something mandatory would not promote the general welfare of the country and the people because making something obligatory actually hurts and forces the people and society by doing something that do not want to do.

General Welfare

While the Affordable Care Act might seem like it promotes the general welfare of people and society, it actually hurts and forces both the former and the latter by pushing down the throats of society and the people of the society. A more useful and better approach would be the United States Congress passing a law to expand Medicare to the rest of the populace, instead of leaving it for the use by people who are sixty-five years and older. Expanding Medicare to the rest of the people would make it better to promote the general welfare of the people and the society, for the good of the country. Providing free college education would also be promoting the general welfare of the society and the people, as it helps further the growth of the country. Now, this might seem like a lot of money, but in the end, it is in line with the originalist interpretation of the constitutional meaning. However, for this to happen, there must be radical changes in how the United States Government operates. Currently, there is government overreach, with massive amounts of abuse and corruption, too many unnecessary government agencies, and a lack of funds due to constant and unnecessary spending. For free college education and the expansion of universal healthcare for everyone, several government agencies must be eliminated. Tax reform also needs to take place, and unnecessary laws need to be repealed and never replaced. Universal healthcare actually promotes the general welfare of the people and the society, and it is in line with the original meaning of the constitution.

Steps to make college free or affordable and to make health insurance affordable

The Federal Bureau of Investigation would be eliminated, as its original intentions were political, basically to keep track of anarchists. It was formed by the attorney general for Theodore Roosevelt, who later became a Progressive politician. Now, anarchy is a political organization, meaning the overthrowing of government with chaos everywhere. Obviously, there remains no need to have some political organization like the FBI exist, even though they say they are apolitical. The FBI is a domestic spy agency. It is an intelligence agency, which means it spies on the people, but not for international reasons, but for domestic. The framers would be rolling in their graves if they were watching the lawlessness of such a government agency.

The Internal Revenue Service would be eliminated, as this agency has abused its power and authority, and actually does not really promote anything but greed and corruption. There is currently a policy in place since the American Civil War known as Citizenship-based taxation. The framers would also be rolling in their graves if they were watching. The framers did not want government to go outside of its jurisdiction to make people pay taxes, they wanted a fair taxation system, one in which that promotes based on residency. If people lived in the jurisdiction of the United States of America, then they should be reasonably taxed. However, if a citizen of the United States of America lived and worked in France or a foreign country outside the jurisdiction of the United States, then they believed taxation is not mandated, since those people are not making taxable income in the United States of America. A fair tax of 15% would replace the current personal income tax system on individuals. Restaurants would charge a 20% Value-added tax. Stores would charge a 5% sales tax. There would be a 15% business tax. The last tax would be a 20% flat tax on imports and exports brought to the United States of America. All other taxes would be eliminated, and this tax system will promote freedom, liberty, prosperity, dreams, and new hope. This will bring in revenues of twenty-five trillion dollars, with less waste and spending. People would be now paying taxes directly to the Department of the Treasury, and this is possible, even with a value added tax. The employees would be working for the Department of the Treasury directly, and not for some quasi-government agency.

The Secret Service would go back to stopping and preventing the use of counterfeiting money, and would become a child agency of the Department of the Treasury.

The Immigration and Customs Enforcement Agency will go back to checking the identities of people and tourists, at both ports, airports, train depots, and border crossings, and would become a child agency of the Department of Justice.

The United States Marshals Service will be the primary federal law enforcement agency in the country, and shall increase by 50% in the first year, and by a steady 5% each year for employment.

All other federal law enforcement agencies would be eliminated, as there is no need for political law enforcement agencies to exist, in order to commit an abuse of power by corruption and by using domestic spying tactics on the populace.

The department of state, department of defense, department of the treasury, and attorney general, including the vice president, would be kept as federal departments to the cabinet of the executive branch. The department of interior, the department of labor, and the department of agriculture would be combined into one department, known as the department of the interior. The department of defense and department of health and human services would be combined into one department, known as the department of defense and health. The department of state would be combined with the department of veteran affairs, known as the department of state, where the department of veterans affairs would become a federal agency. The departments of transportation, energy, labor, veteran affairs, agriculture, commerce, housing and urban development, and homeland security would be eliminated. In total, there would be six cabinet departments, the department of state, the department of defense and health, the department of the treasury, the department of the interior, the department of justice, and the department of education.

Several government agencies and positions will be eliminated from the departments of justice, interior, health, defense, treasury, and other locations.

This would provide for a better society to promote the freedom, liberty, prosperity, hope, and general welfare of the people and the society in the country.

Article One Originalist Interpretation

Section One Originalist Interpretation
Section one of the first article means that the legislative branch shall consist of two branches, and shall be called the Congress of the United States of America, with one branch being named the House of Representatives, and the other being the Senate. This branch has the power and authority to legislate by writing proposed bills, then by sending them to the President to sign them into laws, if applicable.

Section Two Originalist Interpretation
The members of the House of Representatives are elected every two years by the citizens of the populace for each state. The people who choose the members shall be considered electors of that state, which originally was the state legislature. So, it was originally the members of the largest house of each state legislature who voted for the members of the House of Representatives. However, years later, voting was considered a fundamental right for every qualified citizen. Before, citizens were not given the inherent right to vote, but only the members of the state legislature.

To qualify to be a member of the house of representatives, a person must be at least 25 years old, have been a citizen of that particular state for a minimum of seven years, and be living in that state when chosen or elected.

The representatives shall be apportioned across the states. Direct taxes of any kind should also be apportioned across the states. This means that states should get an equal amount of the representatives as well as any revenue made from the federal government. The appropriation was determined by the number of free people, who by chance and luck were Caucasian. Native Americans were excluded from this process as they were not taxed, as well as any slaves, including blacks, whites, and any minorities. Slaves and minorities only counted as three-fifths of a person, so that meant white people were the privileged class in society. The actual process of determining the legal amount of taxable people would begin within three years after the Congress first met. Every ten years there shall be a census or collection of people to determine the appropriate number of members who should be elected for each state to the House of Representatives. For each member elected to the house of representative, each shall have no more or no less than 30,000 constituents. Each state in the union is allowed at least one member to represent that state in the House of Representatives. For national interests, in order to begin the initial process of enumeration, a number of states in the first sitting of Congress received an appropriated amount of members to join the House of Representatives.

If vacancies exist within any state, the governor would issue a special election in order to select a replacement for that particular person.

The members of the House of Representatives will choose their leaders who will take charge in the House of Representatives. The members of the House of Representatives have the power and authority to impeach federal officials who represent the federal government.

Section Three Originalist Interpretation
Each state will have two senators who will represent that state in Congress. Those senators shall serve a term of six years and each one will have one vote. The legislature of each state shall choose the senators for that particular state. However, years later, the citizens of the populace now could vote for the senators.

Elections shall be staggered, where there would be three classes, so that the entire senate would not be elected at the same time. One-third of the senators shall be elected and decided every election cycle, which is every two years. This would prevent chaos. If senators resigned or anything happened to them, during any legislative recess of any state, then the governor of that state shall appoint a replacement for the remainder of that original term, until an election is scheduled.

In order to qualify as a senator, one must be a minimum of thirty years old, be a citizen for nine years minimum of the United States of America, and must live in that state to which he is elected in which he wants to represent.

The Vice President of the United States of America is the President of the Senate, but has no vote, unless it is equally apportioned.

The Senators will choose its officers and party leaders within the Senate to promote leadership. An officer of the Senate will to chosen to replace the Vice President as the Senate President, when the Vice President is absent.

The Senate will be the judge and jury of all impeachments and strict protocols shall be followed. The Senate must make an oath or affirmation in order to take the proceedings seriously. In the case of the presidential impeachment, the chief justice of the Supreme Court shall preside over the proceedings to have a fair and balanced trial. Conviction requires at least two-thirds of the members present.

Any official who was convicted on impeachment would be removed from office and then disqualified from any public office under the United States of America. However, the convicted officials who were impeached could still be liable for civil and criminal punishment.

Section Four Originalist Interpretation
Elections for Senators and members of the House of Representatives shall be decided upon by each state legislature, however, at any time, Congress can change those regulations, except in the location of choosing senators.

Congress is mandated to meet at least once a year, and the first meeting should be the first Monday in December, unless a law is signed to say otherwise. This means that the members of Congress must meet at least one day out of the year as a minimum, where the original date must be the first Monday in December.

Section Five Originalist Interpretation

Both houses of congress shall determine their own elections within Congress. This means that the members of both houses determine if a bill is qualified to proceed from a committee to the general floor of each house. A quorum is conducted just to determine if enough members are present to debate the issue and then vote for or against the proposed bill. Not all members need to be present, but if more members are needed, then the rest of the members will be mandated to attend the debate hearing of the issue concerning the proposed bill, provided that they are present in the capital, and if they are then they could be penalized for not attending.

Each house of Congress can determine their own rules for disciplining their members, where these procedures and guidelines are subject to change. If for some reason a member of any house is constantly disruptive, to the point it interferes in everyday legislation, then that member can be expelled from that house with a minimum of two-thirds of votes from the members of that house.

Each house of Congress must maintain a journal of record in order to keep a paper trail to publish it to the public. Occasionally, the journal shall be published. However, certain entries in the journal can be kept secret, due to interests of national security or other reasons. The members who vote for or against a bill or legislation must be issued into the journal if one-fifth of the members request such an entry, provided a quorum is in place.

Both houses of Congress must declare their intent to adjourn or recess if it last for more than three days. If the Senate wants to adjourn for four days, then they must get consent from the house of representatives, and the same would apply to the house of representatives, since they need to get consent from the Senate. Both houses must meet in the designated location set by Congress. If any house wants to meet in a different location, then that house must seek the consent of the other house.

Section Six Originalist Interpretation

Each member of Congress shall be issued a form of compensation for their public service to the government serving the people of the country. Such compensation might be set into stone by law, and shall be paid by the funds of the Department of the Treasury. Members of Congress have full diplomatic immunity and are immune from being arrested when in attendance, with the exceptions of committing treason, felonies, or disturbing the peace. Members of Congress are immune from arrest and prosecution when giving speeches or debates on the floor of the house, in any house chamber, and the same applies when returning.

Members in Congress may not hold more than one office at the same time. Members of Congress cannot be members of the executive branch or even the judicial system. Members of Congress cannot resign to take a higher salary from a different, new, or higher position, because they must wait until their term ends. Members of Congress, the executive branch, and the judiciary can only hold one office at a time.

Section Seven Originalist Interpretation

Any legislation proposing to raise revenue for the country and government to operate must originate from the House of Representatives. The Senate, however, has the power and authority to propose any amendments of a similar bill in their chamber to have a concurrence of legitimacy.

If a bill passes both house chambers, that proposed bill shall be presented to the President of the United States of America, where if it is approved, then it is signed into public law, but if he objects the bill, it can be returned by being rewritten, overridden by a veto majority, or not reconsidered. The president shall make his objections clear to the house where it originated from if he is against the bill. If Congress decides to reconsider the bill, they may take up the bill to override the presidential veto, and it will become public law if and only if members of both houses of congress vote at least with a two-thirds majority. From the time that Congress submits the bill, the President has ten days to sign it into law, and if it is not signed within or after ten days, then the bill becomes public law. If for some reason the Congress is in recess and the presidents fails to sign the bill into public law within or after ten days, then the Congress cannot override the veto.

Everything passed by Congress must be submitted to the president for approval or rejection, except a question relating to adjournment. It shall become public law if approved. However, it shall become public law if at least two-thirds of the members by both houses of congress decide to override the president's disproval, regarding the rules, regulations, and procedures set by the constitution about legislation.

Section Eight Originalist Interpretation

Congress has the power and authority to determine, propose, and collect taxes, duties, imposts, and excises to pay any debts outstanding for defence and the general welfare of the country, the government, the society, and the people. All duties, imposts, and excises shall be uniform across the United States of America.

Congress has the power and authority to borrow money on behalf of the credit of the United States of America.

Congress has the power and authority to regulate commerce and trade with any foreign entity or foreign nation, amongst the several states of the union, and amongst any Native American tribes.

Congress has the power and authority to establish a uniform proceeding of naturalization and uniform laws regarding bankruptcies, throughout the United States of America.

Congress has the power and authority to coin any form of currency, regulate the value, and to set a fixed standard regarding weights and measures.

Congress has the power and authority to punish counterfeiting of any currency established by the United States of America.

Congress has the power and authority to create and maintain a post office system and post roads.

Congress has the power and authority to promote the progression of any science and the arts. For a limited amount of time, Congress shall grant authors and inventors the exclusive rights to their materials, and that limited amount of time granted to authors and inventors shall be used to promote their products exclusively to inclusive causes.

Congress has the power and authority to create courts and court systems that are below the Supreme Court of the United States of America.

Congress has the power and authority to punish all piracy-related activity relating to the high seas and the bodies of water, within and under the jurisdiction of the United States of America and any offense relating to the international community.

Congress has the power and authority to declare war on foreign nations, to grant approval to capture the enemies of the state, and establish the guidelines to capture the enemies of the state on land and water, within the jurisdiction of the United States of America, and when permission is required, it shall be asked to the other nation to capture, or it would be considered illegal and unlawful.

Congress has the power and authority to appropriate any money amongst the armies for the United States of America, but shall not last for more than two years at a time.

Congress has the power and authority to maintain a navy.

Congress has the power and the authority to make procedures and guidelines for the government and to regulate the land and naval forces within the jurisdiction of the United States of America and when on foreign soil. Congress has the power and the authority to mandate the militia to be ordered to serve in times of insurrections, rebellions, or invasions. This means that Congress can ask for a militia to be organized in order to stop an insurrection, a rebellion, or an invasion within the jurisdiction of the United States of America. An insurrection means that violence has to be present, not just an empty threat of intimidation or coercion. Violence needs to actually take place. If violence does not exist, then it is not an insurrection. An insurrection is a reckless act of violence that seeks to destroy the very uniform rule of law by killing people with no regard to the law, promoting intimidation against the United States of America, and by using coercion to get things done. All three of these conditions must be met in order for it to be an insurrection. An invasion is when a country or an enemy state decides to attack the United States of America. A rebellion means that people are rebelling against the government, but this rebellion might be justified if the citizens are trying to stop a tyrannical and corrupted government who refuse to respect the constitution.

Congress has the power and authority to organize, arming, and disciplining the militia when necessary. The members may be service men within the United States of America or be in reserved at the state level respectively. The appointment of officers and the duty of training regarding discipline remains under the control of procedures adopted by the Congress.

Congress has the power and the authority to exercise exclusive legislation in any case over districts in order to make those particular places the seat of the government of the United States of America. The federal government will have jurisdiction over this district and shall create and establish any necessary government buildings and infrastructures, by purchasing the amount of no more than ten square miles. Congress also has the power and authority to purchase land in the states in order to build necessary buildings, infrastructures, and anything else deemed necessary, under the consent and permission of the state legislature. This means that the state must consent the land to the federal government if the latter wants to purchase and use it for government purposes. The federal government cannot just seize the land; they must seek the permission and consent from the state legislature where that land is located.

Congress has the power and authority to make all laws passed to be enforced within the jurisdiction of the United States of America, under the constitution. The government cannot enforce their laws outside the jurisdiction of the power of the United States of America. If the government tries to enforce their law in a foreign country not under the jurisdiction of the United States of America, then it is considered unconstitutional. The United States government only has jurisdiction over the fifty states, the commonwealths, and the territories of the United States of America, but does not have jurisdiction over any foreign nation or any associated state

Section Nine Originalist Interpretation

No law concerning migration or importation of people being brought into the states in the union shall be created until the year 1808, but for revenue reasons, a tax or duty can be imposed on such migration or importation of such an act, not to exceed more than ten dollars. This clause relates to the issue of slavery and the slave trade.

Habeas Corpus, or the act of reporting illegal detention or imprisonment of an individual, shall not be suspended, unless the country and government is under attack from an armed rebellion or an armed insurrection promoting violence, committing acts of violence, by using coercion and intimidation, in order to promote a lawless society with chaos everywhere.

No law declaring people guilty without a trial shall be passed by any part of the legislative branches or by anyone in government itself. No law may change the consequences to a harsher penalty after a penalty has been issued against the parties who committed the alleged acts. Such acts are illegal and unconstitutional due to the fact that it would be based on material opinion and that someone already received a consequence, but then another law passed, making that consequence obsolete and instituting a harsher punishment.

There shall be no payments of fees or any other direct taxes established unless the proportion from the census is equal to the amount before it is directed to be taken. This means that taxation must be in proportion with the census.

There shall be no law created relating to the taxation or duty laid on articles for the use of exportation from any state. This means that states exporting goods and services to other states within the United States of America will not pay any fee to the federal government.

No port shall be given special treatment for any regulation regarding commerce or revenue, regardless of the state where it is located. No vessels are bound or mandated to enter, clear, or pay duties to another port in another state.

No funds from the department of the treasury shall be withdrawn, except in the consequences of appropriations enacted by law. Records of receipts and frequent statements from the accounts of expenditures of all public money shall be published in an occasional manner.

There shall be no title of nobility granted by the United States of America. No person holding public office may be issued any title of nobility, title, gift, or office from any King, Queen, or Prince of any foreign nation, without the approval of the Congress. People holding public office prior to and after their terms may be issued these titles.

Section Ten Originalist Interpretation
No state of the union may enter into foreign relations, an alliance, a treaty, or a confederation with any other foreign nation. No state of the union may grant or issue letters of non-prosecution for the use of employing privateers into combating the enemy for any reason. No state of the union may coin or print currency, can make bills of credit, but may issue or create gold and silver currency coin or tender for the use of paying debts. No state of the union may pass any law relating to the destruction of due process, make

any law related to impairing obligatory contracts, or grant any title of nobility.

No state of the union may issue or establish any imposts or duties on imports or exports, without the consent and approval from Congress, with the exception of what might be necessary to execute inspection laws. Any duties or imposts established by any state on imports or exports shall be reserved for the usage of the Department of the Treasury of the United States of America, and all laws shall be subject to revision and regulation for control by the Congress, for the net produce received.

No state of the union may issue or establish any duty of tonnage, keep troops or ships of war during peace, may enter into a compact or treaty with any other state or foreign nation, or engage in war, without approval from the consent of Congress. At the same time, no state of the union may engage in any war-like behavior unless invaded. A state may engage in war in the case of imminent danger.

Article Two Originalist Interpretation

Section One Originalist Interpretation

The president of the United States of America is the official executive of the government and holds the power of all executive power within the reach of their power and authority granted by the constitution. Each term is limited to four years. The vice president is chosen at the same time as the president, unless there is a contested nomination process, but both positions in the executive branch serve together in the same term.

Each state that is part of the union is obligated to appoint qualified people as electors to appoint the president and vice president of the United States of America. This process is conducted by each state legislature. This process is completely determined by the states. The number of electors must be proportional to the amount of current members in Congress. There is a restriction of people who cannot be electors, such as members of Congress and any person holding public office within and under the power and authority of the United States of America.

The electors shall only meet in their states to which they are citizens of and reside in. Each elector voted for two people to be the next president of the United States of America, but one of the nominees must reside in and be a citizen of another state who is not from the same state as the elector. A list of people voted to be the president shall be compiled and recorded, with necessary certification of the process, signed, and then sent to seat the two newly elected officials to power at the seat of government, which is taken up by the current president of the senate before it can be confirmed. The current president of the senate, with the presence of all members of Congress, must read the certifications, which will then be counted for votes to determine the president and the vice president. The person with the highest amount of votes will become the president if a majority of electors chose that person as president, and the person with the second highest would become vice president. If there is a tie between the candidates and no majority is received for a single nominee, then the house of representatives will choose the next president who tied with each other from the nominees with the five highest votes, while the senate will choose the vice president after the house of representatives choose the president, and disregards the president of taking him off of the list, now leaving the second person who received the next highest amount of votes to be vice president. But, in the case of a second tie, the senate will choose who, from the tied candidates, who would become the next vice president. Each state has one equal vote. A quorum will be required where at least two-thirds of the states must have at least one member of congress in attendance. The majority of the states shall partake in this process to determine choice.

Congress is the sole body with the only power and authority who may determine when the electors will be chosen and how they will be chosen. On that designated day, the electors are obligated to cast their votes, and shall be uniform and the same day across the United States of America.

To be qualified as President, a person must be born within the jurisdiction of the United States of America or be a natural-born citizen of a genetic relationship from a person or relationship with at least one member of that genetic trait being a citizen of the United States of America. Each qualified person must be at least thirty-five years of age when he takes the oath of office and must be a resident of at least fourteen years within the jurisdiction of the United States of America. This is important because the framers did not want some foreign dignitary becoming the executive because of a fear of abuse of power by the British government at the time.

If the president is deemed unfit for office, whether regarding death, resigning, or refuse or unable to follow his duties of the executive office, then he shall be removed, with the same being applied to the vice president. If such a case arises, the Congress shall make a case to remove that executive from power and replacing him with the vice president, provided that the vice president meets all qualifications to become president, regarding the issue of death, resignation, or refusal or unabledness to be a sound or effective president. Congress may, however, set a line of succession. During this process, the case shall be decided who is qualified to be the next president and vice president, until if and when the problem is resolved. That person who replaces the predecessor shall serve until the next election. If that replacement is chosen during the next presidential election to become president, then he shall remain in office for the next four years in power.

The president of the United States of America is entitled to compensation or payments for his services performed, and it shall not increase nor decrease during the time he is in office for which he was elected for. He is not entitled to any other payment from any other office within the United States of America, for which when he was elected into office of the president of the United States of America.

The president must take an oath of office by either agreeing or stating the oath of the swearing before he can begin his duties of being the president of the United States of America.

Section Two Originalist Interpretation

The president of the United States of America is the executive in charge of the army and naval forces of the country, as well as the executive in charge of all state-sanctioned militias when those state-sanctioned militias are called into duty of the United States of America. Each state executive may be obligated, if necessary, to give their opinions to the issue regarding the state-sanctioned militia to the president, relating to the obligatory duties of their office within the state governments. The president can also grant clemency or pardon any person who committed an act against or within the United States of America, except for when someone is being impeached.

The president has the power to create and establish treaties, also known as international compacts or agreements between government, only with the consent and approval by the Senate. Two-thirds of the Senators must agree to the proposed treaty in order for it to be valid, legal, and constitutional. This means that if a president or an agency of the executive branch signs an international agreement with governments without the consent and approval of the Senate, then the proposed treaty is invalid, illegal, and unconstitutional under the constitution. The president shall also have the power and authority to appoint any ambassador and dignitaries to consulates or missions, judges to any court and the supreme court, and to any other public office within and under the jurisdiction of the United States of America, with advice and consent from the Senate, meaning if the appointment is the correct choice for that particular public office. The executive in charge of each department or the courts also have the power and authority to appoint, if necessary, with the same criteria from the Senate.

If there is a vacancy, the president has the power and authority to make recess appointments during the adjournment of the Senate, but these appointments are temporary. The appointments made during the recess of the Senate will be either confirmed or denied by the Senate, before their next session ends. The president is not obligated to appoint people if there is a vacancy, but simply has the power and authority to do so.

Section Three Originalist Interpretation

The president should occasionally present information to Congress concerning the current state of the union, regarding policies, future policies, how policies are being instituted, and what is being done, as well as what is being considered to confront these issues or concerns. The president shall make recommendations to Congress regarding certain issues, as he sees fit and judges them accordingly for their merit. In certain circumstances, the president has the power and authority to convene both or either houses of congress, and if there is disagreement between the meeting date and time, he has the power and authority to adjournment both or either house of congress until a future date and time can be agreed upon. The president will receive and determine all dignitaries of consulates and missions as well as the cabinet members, also known as the department heads of each department in the executive branch, which is regarding the use of domestic and foreign policy matters. The president should enforce all laws mandated by congress, but if he believes a law is unconstitutional that violates the rules and principles of the constitution, he shall not enforce those laws after a process of deep-thinking analysis. The president has the power and authority to commission all officers within and under the jurisdiction of the United States of America, who are employed by the United States of America.

Section Four Originalist Interpretation

Any public official of the federal government, regardless if elected or not elected, can be removed from that office by impeachment, if they are convicted on an issue relating to treason, bribery, felonious acts, or any misdemeanor.

Article Three Originalist Interpretation

Section One Originalist Interpretation

The judicial power is controlled by the Supreme court of the United States of America, as well as courts inferior to the supreme court. The number of courts inferior to the supreme court can be unlimited or limited, as congress determines the number of inferior courts that shall exist. All judges to the supreme court and its inferior counterparts must serve in good standing, meaning that they must act accordingly to the constitution, the law, and ability to serve. As judges, they shall be compensated for their public service of the government, and this compensation shall not decrease while in office.

Section Two Originalist Interpretation

The power of the judiciary applies to all cases, regarding law and equality, domestic law, the agreements between the United States government and foreign nations, which is under the authority and mentioned in the constitution. Any case of law regarding ambassadors, foreign ministers, consuls, or cabinet officials shall also face the judicial power of law and equality, domestic law, and the agreements between the United States government and foreign nations, and shall also be extended to all cases concerning admiralty and maritime jurisdiction, where the United States government is a party in name. This shall also be applied to cases regarding the law and equality between two or more states, between the citizens of another state and a particular state, as well as with between citizens of different states, with between citizens of their own state claiming lands under grants that belong to other states, between a state-to-state conflict or conflicts between the citizens of those states, and including foreign entities not under the control of the government, regarding citizens or their subjects. This means that the judiciary power applies to all cases regarding law and equality amongst domestic law, treaty law, maritime law, instituted law, and anything regarding the United States of

America, extending to everyone, including public officials, to conflicts between citizens and states, conflicts between states, and conflicts between foreign entities and citizens, if it happens within the jurisdiction of the United States of America, which must be on U.S. soil, or be about concerns related to US law and policy, but all cases that are heard must be not yet decided upon before or must be risen to the question of a potential concern to the public of society.

The Supreme Court has original jurisdiction over concerns relating to ambassadors, consuls, and public ministers of the government, as well as the cases concerning in which a state is a party of a main issue. The other cases, not mentioned, the supreme court is considered the appellate jurisdiction relating to law, truth, and evidence, relating to these exceptions, but under the guidance of legislation and procedures passed by Congress.

Any criminal case, except for impeachment, is heard by a jury, where the trial will be located in the state where said crime was committed. If a crime was not committed in any particular state, the trial shall be located where congress deems as appropriate, with an appropriate date, place, and time, with regard to law or legislation deemed by Congress.

Section Three Originalist Interpretation

Treason is defined as declaring or conducting war against the United States of America, or to be in allegiance with the enemy of the government, including granting aid and or comfort. A person will only be convicted of treason if two witnesses of the same act have testified to the truthfulness of the claims, or if the defendant confesses to the crime in an open court during trial or a trial proceeding such as arraignment.

Congress determines the overall punishment for treason. However, a trial must be conducted to determine the outcome, and any heirs to that person being tried cannot lose any part of their possible inheritance, even if that person is convicted. Congress may take the convicted traitor's property, but that property must transfer to the heir when the convicted person died, if such an heir exists. This means congress must return the property to any heirs when the traitor dies.

Article Four Originalist Interpretation

Section One Originalist Interpretation

Each state must recognize the results of cases in other states as a reciprocity agreement between all states, regarding criminal cases, civil cases, and all judicial proceedings of any kind. The exception would be getting a judgement in one state but enforcing it in a different state. The state where the judgment originated must be enforced in that state, before it can be enforced in any other state. This is known as procedural law. If a party gets a judgment from a court in one jurisdiction but wants to enforce it in any other state before the originated state, then it would be unconstitutional. If a party gets a judgment from a court in one jurisdiction but only wants to enforce it in a different state jurisdiction, then it is also unconstitutional. It must first be enforced in the state jurisdiction of where it originated in order to be recognized, and then it can be enforced in other states. Congress has the power and authority to pass legislation to decide how this process might work or be determined, for the use of regulation.

Section Two Originalist Interpretation

All citizens of the United States of America are entitled to equal protection and privileges, regardless of their home state. This means that all citizens are entitled to all immunities, privileges, and rights of the United States of America and all of the states. This includes freedom of movement as well as any transaction, regardless if it is interstate or in the residing state. All states must recognize and grant the immunities, protection, and privileges to the citizens of the United States of America, where all citizens are entitled to equal protection.

If a person who was charged with any type of crime, regardless of the nature, including treason, felony, and misdemeanor, and has escaped justice by running away to face the judicial system, then that person shall be extradited to the state where the crime was committed, if the person is found in a different state. This means that if a person charged with a crime escapes the judicial system where the crime was committed then that person will be extradited back to that state if he is found hiding in a different state.

A person who is in service of labor to one party in one state shall not be dismissed from service if found in a different state, but that person who is in service of labor to that party will be returned to that party if found and captured. This has mostly to do with slaves who escaped their masters and were found in other states.

Section Three Originalist Interpretation

New states can be admitted to the United States of America, but there are some strict stipulations. A new state cannot be within the jurisdiction of a current state. A new state cannot be formed of the border of two or more states or even part of states. If a new state is to be formed under these guidelines stated, then they need permission from the state legislatures where it shall be formed as well as the consent and approval of Congress.

Congress has the power and authority to dispose of any land and also can establish any rules and regulations regarding that land, territory, or property belonging to the United States of America. However, the government must respect the territory where the property or land is located. The government cannot, however, harm the states where the claim is made for the land. The government has the power and authority to manage authority and cannot be harmed for any claim made. Nevertheless, this does not give the government the right to buy and own land, but just to manage it. The government cannot seize any land because it wants that particular parcel of land, as that is unconstitutional. The government has the power and authority to own certain types of land, properties, infrastructures, and territories, but cannot just claim a particular parcel it wants. Neither the states nor the federal government can be harmed relating to the disposal or purchase of land, but the federal government must respect the land and property in the state where it is located, as well as the sovereign status of that particular state.

Section Four Originalist Interpretation

Each state in and under jurisdiction of the United States of America shall have a Republican form of government, where the government will protect each state equally from any invasions. If the legislative branch of that state cannot be convened during times of domestic violence, then the executive branch of that state shall take control of the matter.

Article Five Originalist Interpretation

Whenever two-thirds of members of both houses of congress demand a change to the constitution, amendments shall be proposed and be taken into consideration. Amendments to the constitution can also be considered whenever two-thirds of the state legislatures decide to call a constitutional convention for such proposed amendments. In order for the proposed amendment(s) to be valid and be ratified, there are two choices to take. Three-fourths of the states in the United States of America must ratify it by their state legislature, or three-fourths of the states in the United States of America must ratify it at a state ratification convention. The method of choice for ratification is chosen by Congress. No amendment can be made, proposed, or ratified before 1808, affecting or regarding the issues in the first and fourth clauses in the ninth section of the first article. No state can be denied its equality in the Senate unless consent is granted by that state. Suffrage means the right to vote, so this means that no state can or will lose their senators ability to vote on issues unless that state agrees to withdraw from the voting process, as well as the equal amount of seats held by each state for the senate.

Article Six Originalist Interpretation

The debts that were issued before the current constitution are still valid and must be paid. The Articles of the Confederation was the first constitution of the United States of America. All outstanding debts issued to the government during the time and life of the articles of confederation are all valid and must be paid, according to the constitution agreed to upon at the constitutional convention.

The constitution of the United States of America agreed to upon at the constitutional convention, as well as the legislation passed by congress then signed into law by the president, and any international agreements between made between foreign nations and governments are the supreme law of the land. All judges who hold office under and in the jurisdiction of the United States of America, including state and federal, are bound by these laws, the entire constitution, and state laws are subordinate to federal law. The constitution is a law, where the state constitutions are subordinate to the United States constitution.

All members of congress, all members of the state legislatures, all members of the executive branch in federal and state office, and all members of the judicial branch in state and federal office are bounded by an oath or affirmation to the United States constitution, to support and uphold it. There is no religious test that will be mandated for any person holding public office within and under the jurisdiction of the United States of America, including federal and state office holders.

Article Seven Originalist Interpretation

At the time of the original proposal of the constitution, nine out of the thirteen states had to agree to ratify the constitution, in order for it to be effectively passed as the law of the land. Nine states were sufficient enough for ratification. The framers at the constitutional convention believed nine states were enough to pass and ratify the constitution into law.

Bill of Rights Constitutional Interpretation

The Bill of Rights as it was Originally Interpreted

Written by
Edna Faust

First Amendment Originalist Interpretation

When writing the first amendment to the constitution, the framers did not want the government to force a religion down the throats of the populace. The government in England at the time forced a form of Christianity down the throats of their populace. In this new society being proposed, all religions were equal amongst society. No religion was the official religion of the populace and everyone was free to go to any church they wanted. The framers wanted the people to have free speech, no matter what was said. The framers understood that governments in other countries do restrict speech and they believed it was wrong. The framers wanted the people and the news media to say what they wanted even though if disagreements were made. The government did not want to restrict your thoughts or what anyone or any entity said about anyone or anything else. The framers wanted everyone and everything to express their feelings, and to express those feelings when people believed that the government or someone or something else was committing a wrong.

Second Amendment Originalist Interpretation

The second amendment seems to be the most controversial in existence. It is constantly interpreted differently by liberals and conservatives, where the liberals interpret it with condemnation, as they see it as a threat to their beliefs. The amendment states forth a militia. Now, this militia must be well-regulated, meaning it must be strictly controlled by the leaders and the members of the militia. Now, there are generally two types of militia, one operated by the state governments under the control of the United States of America and the one formed by citizens. The latter usually is created to combat tyranny and meets in secret. Both of these militias have to defend the constitution. This amendment also allows the militia the right to have weapons, as well as the citizens of the United States of America to have weapons. The people and the militia are allowed to own and use weapons, and those rights cannot be restricted. The militia is the citizenry of the free state. The purpose of the militia is to keep the government in check. If the militia overthrows the government, then it is treason. No militia wants to overthrow the government unless they want to disregard the rule of law. The militia is not a military, but an organization of people who try to bring peace and order back to society.

Third Amendment Originalist Interpretation

The framers did not want the government to invade peoples' home and or place of residence. No soldier can mandate that a person allow them to live there. The only exception is when a soldier asks permission and the owner agrees. It is unconstitutional and illegal for a soldier to live in a home without the owner's or tenant's permission, unless he is the true owner or renter of that property.

Fourth Amendment Originalist Interpretation

People have the right to privacy. The government or any government agency does not have any right to spy or stalk people, unless a specific warrant is issued for a specific reason. The government or any government agency does not have any right to issue a broad warrant with unlimited names and unlimited reasons. A specific cause must be stated. Everything must be specific in the warrant and a warrant must be specific and be issued to search and or seize property and individuals.

Fifth Amendment Originalist Interpretation

If people are called upon to answer a question relating to a capital offense or some other type of heinous crime, then they must be indicted by a grand jury if evidence exists, with the exception being in times of land or naval forces and of that of the militia, during the time of war or of public danger, when in service. This means that soldiers in the military and members of a government militia are not protected by the grand jury, so no indictment or grand jury is needed to charge that person. The government does not have the right to retry a person on the same charges if found innocent on charges, of the particular charges found innocent. If a person is convicted on one crime, but acquitted on another, then the government cannot retry that person on the acquitted crime. If a jury is deadlocked and could not reach a decision, then there is a mistrial, where the government can retry the case in probable time. The government or anyone representing the government cannot force people to testify against themselves in a criminal trial. People who are being tried in a criminal trial cannot and will not be deprived of their life, their liberty, or their property, and due process must take place. Any type of private property that is pursued, the government or other entity must pay a reasonable amount of money.

Sixth Amendment Originalist Interpretation

Everyone and every entity being prosecuted and tried in a criminal trial has the right to a fast as possible and public trial, where the jury must be neutral to both parties of the trial to determine the evidence. The trial shall take place in the jurisdiction of the state where the crime took place. Everyone and everything being prosecuted and tried has the right to know why and for what reason they are being tried, and the cause of the reason for the prosecution or trial. The accused shall confront the witnesses during trial and prosecution and can mandate by their attorney to make the witnesses appear in open court to testify. Any accused has the right to have their own favorable witnesses. Any and all accused have the right to effective and assistance for their defense.

Seventh Amendment Originalist Interpretation

In civil cases where monetary damages exceed twenty dollars, a jury trial is mandated. It is unconstitutional for a former civil case to be re-examined in any court by a judge. If it were to be re-examined, it must be filed by the original parties involved and they must motion the court system to re-open the case, where it would usually be examined by a different judge and a different jury. The judge cannot overrule or re-examine the jury's verdict regarding the issue of the facts of evidence related to the jury determining factual determination after the jury has reached its verdict.

Eight Amendment Originalist Interpretation

Excessive bail is unconstitutional. Excessive fines are unconstitutional. Cruel and unusual punishments are unconstitutional. If the accused have an excessive amount of bail for which it is hard to secure, then it is unconstitutional. This means that if your net worth is ten million dollars but your bail is set above that amount, then it would be unconstitutional because it deprives you of your wealth. If the accused committed a crime but the bail is higher than normal, then the bail is unconstitutional, such as if you commit petty theft but is associated with Ponzi schemes or murder. A fine is excessive when it deprives you of your wealth when it reduces your net worth to a standard of living to which you cannot afford to live in a safe or confined environment, such as your own home or a jail. If the fine reduces your net worth by at least fifty percent or at a cost where you could no longer afford to live in a safe and controlled environment, then it would be unconstitutional. Cruel and unusual punishment would be if you committed a crime but the sentence does not match the crime, because the sentence is too harsh. If someone is convicted of arson but is tried under a terrorism law, and the sentence requires something mandatory that is too harsh, then the sentence is cruel and unusual. Usually, arson is not terrorism, but the government has abused its power and authority before, just to make an example out of people. Sometimes, the government attempts to fabricate the evidence by lying. At other times, the government accuses a person or entity of a crime, but no crime ever took place, which would also make that sentence unconstitutional. If a judgment takes away an amount of your net worth, to which you no longer can afford to live in a safe and confined environment, then it is cruel and unusual punishment, making it unconstitutional.

Ninth Amendment Originalist Interpretation

The powers stated in the constitution of certain rights cannot be undermined by the federal government, where those rights cannot be denied or restricted. The federal government cannot increase their power to which they are not entitled to. The federal government cannot undermine the rights of the people guaranteed under the constitution.

Tenth Amendment Originalist Interpretation

The federal government is not entitled to the powers guaranteed to the states. The federal government is not entitled to the powers guaranteed to the people of the United States of America. The federal government must respect the powers and rights guaranteed to the states and the people of the United States of America. The states and the people must respect the powers and rights guaranteed to the federal government. Each entity, the federal government, the states, and the people of the United States of America, must respect the power and rights guaranteed to them under the constitution. There is to be no undermining of any guaranteed powers or rights of any party mentioned.

Afterward

This copy of the constitution, the bill of rights, the amendments, and the declaration of independence was written so that you, the reader, would understand the original intent and meaning of the text. The founders and framers of the United States of America wanted government to have a limited role, not like the government and country they were seceding from. They knew that government must not control people's lives and they did not want government to over regulate its people and the laws.

An abuse of power was known to them, and they wanted to stop it from happening to them, but their original intention was never to create a country and government of their own. The founders and framers of the United States of America wanted to create a country only because they grew tired of the British government and King George.

Throughout this copy of the constitution, the bill of rights, the amendments, and the declaration of independence, there was an intention to stop government over reach. Freedom and liberty is under attack, and is attacked continuously by both the Republicans and the Democrats, as well as by Neocons and the establishment politicians. These politicians could rewrite the constitution because they do not like what it says, they do not like the original meaning, and they believe it to be alive and progressive.

The citizens of the United States of America must care about their freedoms, rights, and liberties, since the government has created tyranny, because they (the government) interprets the laws and constitution differently when a Democrat takes control. When a Republican takes control of the Presidency, the laws and the constitution are taken into context of their original meaning, but the same is not true for Democrats. Democrats will prosecute for political motivations, but so will Republicans; however, Republicans do not prosecute for political motivations as much as the Democrats. As a reader of this book, you should now understand why the constitution was written, and why it must be interpreted as written back in the eighteenth century. Aside from the fact the constitution, the bill of rights, and the declaration of independence are cherished, there remains an important conversation that must happen, the conversation regarding the original intention of the constitution itself.

There are some amendments, such as the sixteenth amendment, that promotes greed and corruption being transmitted to the federal government instead of appropriation. The original plan was to apportion taxes between the states, due to the fact that the framers believed that a government with too much power could be too authoritarian. Greed can be considered as a way of power for the government to control the people and to use tyranny against the people and the rest of society. The eighteenth amendment is also something interesting, which promoted a selfish altitude regarding the issue of alcohol. The eighteenth amendment made alcohol illegal, and if the framers were watching, they would be rolling in their graves. The eighteenth and sixteenth amendment both represent a tactic of selfishness to promote for certain reasons of control. The government does not want people to freedom and liberty, and once a government has a new power, it is hard to abolish that new power, unless a new era of true freedom and liberty rise above by running for office and winning.

At least the rest of the amendments are not as bad, those two amendments would be considered unconstitutional by the framers of the constitution, because they believed too much power was a threat to freedom, liberty, society, and the people.

www.ingramcontent.com/pod-product-compliance
Lightning Source LLC
Chambersburg PA
CBHW032119280326
41933CB00009B/909